I0165286

Moments to Remember

Life-Journey Junctions, Encounters, Revelations

Robert Serpell

Copyright © 2025 Robert Serpell

No part of this book may be reproduced, distributed, or transmitted in any form or by any means, including photocopying, recording, or other electronic or mechanical methods, without the prior written permission of the publisher and the author, except in the case of brief quotations used in reviews or certain other non-commercial uses permitted by copyright law.

Publisher: Upway Books
Author: Robert Serpell
Title: Moments to Remember: Life-Journey Junctions, Encounters, Revelations
ISBN: 978-1-917916-31-8
Cover Designed on Canva: www.canva.com
Cover Image: Robert Serpell

This book is a work of non-fiction. The information it contains is based on the author's research, experience, and knowledge at the time of publication. The publisher and authors have made every effort to ensure the accuracy and reliability of the information provided, but assume no responsibility for any errors, omissions, or differing interpretations of the subject matter. This publication is not intended to replace professional advice or consultation. Readers are encouraged to seek professional guidance where appropriate.

contact@upwaybooks.com
www.upwaybooks.com

Acknowledgements

The literate practice of personal narrative was first introduced to me by my mother Estelle Serpell in my adolescence when she encouraged me to share ideas and feelings in letters posted between our separate locations in London and Singapore, launching a strand of correspondence that extended from the late 1950s to the 2010s, enriching our relationship with glimpses of one another's experiences and reflections on their aesthetic and moral connotations.

In the 1990s, my studies of child development in varied sociocultural contexts brought me into contact with the notion of story-telling as an emerging manifestation of cognitive competence, elaborated by Jerome Bruner, Peggy Miller, Shirley Bryce Heath and others[1].

---

[1] Bruner, J.S. (1986). *Actual minds, possible worlds*. Cambridge University Press.
Miller, P. J., Potts, R., Fung, H., Hoogstra, L., & Mintz, J. (1990). Narrative practices and the social construction of self in childhood. *American Ethnologist*, *17*(2), 292-311.
Heath, S. B. (1983). *Ways with words: Language, life and work in communities and classrooms*. Cambridge University Press.

In the 1990s, as I began to retire from academic life, the idea of writing reflexively about reminiscences of my own life-journey was prompted by correspondence with my friend Francois Rochat, and further energised by an invitation from Frank Kessel to contribute to an edited collection of essays[2].

The present collection was most immediately prompted by a globally distributed discussion arising from my public lecture, hosted by Sumaya Laher in the University of Witwatersrand's *Umthombo* series, entitled "Autoethnography as a source of understanding of life-span human development". I am especially grateful to the following participants in that discussion for encouraging me to make these informally reflective essays more widely accessible in print: Evangeline Danseco, Susan Hill, Francois Rochat and Pamela Wadende. They are, of course, not responsible for the content of the essays, which I hope will resonate with other readers and provoke enlightening reflections on similarities, differences and connections with their own life experiences.

---

[2] Kessel, F. (Ed) (2025). *Pillars of Developmental Psychology: recollections and reflections.* Cambridge University Press.

Table of contents

Introduction

My goal in bringing together this collection of short essays (a complement to my 2024 autobiographical book, *In search of integrity*) is to analyse some personal experiences that stand out as uniquely significant in the course of my life. Some of them are best characterised as remarkable **encounters**, some as moments of **revelation** (or epiphany), and some as intrinsically connected with momentous **junctures** in my life-journey symbolically representative of the decision I took in that moment or episode to orient my life in a new direction.

Each essay is an account of my personal experience of a particular event, situated in time and place, with reflections on its connection with one or more of the philosophical preoccupations articulated in my autobiography. Those were the values of **inclusion and tolerance, rejecting interpersonal violence, aesthetic appreciation, forming intimate relationships of trust**, and **taking responsibility.** In my concluding search for integration, I invoked the concept of

participatory appropriation of an intimate culture of which an individual becomes an **accepted member** and of whose **system of meanings** she or he becomes an **owner**, and thus also an authority. A key factor in the successful attainment of such membership/ownership of a new intimate culture is, I believe, the process of **listening respectfully** (described in section 6 of the book). On the plane of **global social change**, I affirm the hopeful conviction that **progress** is in principle achievable by promoting **inclusion and tolerance** among the diverse cultures that separate human groups from one another.

My personal developmental life-journey, described in the book, took me from a childhood (1944-56) and adolescence (1957-61) in London, through two seminal sojourns in my emerging adulthood first in Singapore (1961-62) and then in Oxford, UK (1962-65), followed by migration at the age of 21 to the newly independent sovereign state of Zambia.

My identity as a "citizen of the world" was nurtured in childhood and adolescence by my liberal-minded, cosmopolitan parents, grounded in a bilingual primary education and international travel. In emerging adulthood in Singapore on the brink of independence, my political awareness was provoked by exposure to the hypocrisy of colonial social practices. In Oxford I devoted much of my efforts to student activism to combat racial oppression through anti-discriminatory legislation in UK and international pressure for de-colonisation in Africa. Concurrently, my academic studies focused on the linguistic approach to epistemology promoted by Wittgenstein and JL Austin, but on a positivist, natural scientific approach to psychology. The first essay in the present collection focuses on an opportunity that came my way during my sojourn at Oxford: **godparenthood**. Invited by a college friend to make a public commitment to take up and honour that role, I experienced some ambivalence about doing so in the ritual language of the established Church of England. I discuss how the linguistic philosophy of Wittgenstein and Austin, that I was studying in the university curriculum, afforded a rationalisation that appealed to me at the time, namely that the significance of my verbal utterance was primarily performative, allowing me to communicate sincerely to the parents of the child being baptised that I was making a serious commitment to "being there for" her in years to come, while bracketing as irrelevant my private misgivings about the epistemological adequacy of the ritual text. Sadly, I never had an opportunity to fulfil that commitment in practice, as the life journeys of my friend and mine diverged to different continents and we lost touch.

Two notable experiences are described in my book as revelatory with respect to the disposition I developed early in life to reject interpersonal violence. The first was framed as a sporting event at school: a boxing match, in which, to my horror, I inflicted on my opponent a massive nosebleed. This prompted a purposeful declaration that was accepted by my family:

"That I would never again participate in the heinous sport of boxing. ...It was just accepted that Robbie does not like boxing, does not watch boxing matches, and certainly doesn't box himself. "(p 19)

The second was the Headmaster's violent caning of a group of us boys aged 14-16, framed as ritual punishment for a forbidden recreational misbehaviour in the school grounds. This abusive exercise of power in the name of adult authority and its inhumane endorsement by the school matron prompted a juncture in my life-journey at which I severed my relationship with the school.

The principle of taking responsibility emerged in the wake of leaving school, but only acquired urgency at the crisis of my confrontation with my father in early adulthood in Singapore. The substance of the meeting, as described in my book, came as a shock. But reflection on our relationship over the preceding months suggests that in a way I expected it. The experience forced me to acknowledge that I could only justify defying my parents' intrusion into my romantic attachment by proving to them, and to myself, that I could manage the basic economy of my subsistence by earning an income.

The most salient juncture in my life-journey was informed by the decision in 1965 to move with my recently married partner to Zambia. It was prompted by an unusual convergence of my existing political and psychological interests represented by a job opportunity advertised on a *3x5-inch index card*, discussed in the second essay in this collection. The coherence of my reasoning in deciding to apply might suggest that the direction I took was optimally planned, but a positive outcome was not predictable at the time. It came about as a result of many later events. Four years later, I was disappointed with the meagre insights achieved in my doctoral thesis on experimental psychological studies of Zambian children's perception and learning. My marriage had collapsed, but had brought into the world my first child, with whom I was excitingly engaged. The third essay, *This is a nice house*, illustrates our relationship with the story of a revealing conversation between us while traveling.

Reflection on the shortcomings of my research led me to embark on a different kind of project that involved listening respectfully and connecting locally (discussed in section 6 of the book). Meanwhile, I was fortunate to forge a new romantic relationship that blossomed into an enduring partnership with my spouse Namposya. The fourth essay, **The slice of pizza**, describes how the indigenous celebration of our wedding gave rise to an epiphany treasured by both of us over the years, highlighting the imperative of sharing for a social partnership between two individuals to endure.

The next four essays focus on events in a ten-year period during which our partnership expanded to include three more children, and we travelled for sojourns that lasted between a few weeks and more than a year in various different sociocultural settings around the world: Honolulu, Washington DC, Hull UK, and Malawi. None of those events were associated with such a dramatic juncture in my life journey as joining the University of Zambia in 1965. But each of them resonates with one or more of my major, overarching, philosophical preoccupations.

The **Jive talk** that mystified the traffic policeman in Honolulu was one of many occasions in which our diverse little family inclusively transcended the stereotypes that tend to keep contrasting cultural groups apart.

The barman's repartee (**What kind of nuts?**) signified my competence-based exclusion in the transactions on Gallaudet University campus in DC, and that enabled me to empathise more profoundly with children alienated from their intimate culture of origin by insufficiently sensitive, well-meaning forms of pedagogy.

The offensive **graffiti** in Hull prompted me to take responsibility for a small-scale corrective intervention, serendipitously affording an opportunity to build a new level of trust into my relationship with my adolescent son.

And the revelatory experience of **The pot of gold** in Malawi generated an aesthetic appreciation by each of the children that served as a memorable feature of our little family's intimate culture.

The final three essays date from later years of my biological life. The painting of *Les Signares* first captured my admiration on aesthetic grounds during a short visit to Senegal in 2009. The artist's explanation of its title triggered a wide-ranging exploration of the cultural-historical processes through which the tragic context of trans-Atlantic slavery was transformed over generations into an elite sub-culture of freed women and men of mixed ethnic heritage. My reflections highlight the paradoxical juxtaposition of moral tragedy with aesthetic beauty that has generated some of the great visual art and literature of history around the world, affording a humanistic perspective on progressive social change.

Boda-boda describes a revelatory encounter on another short trip abroad in my 70s. The phenomenon of motorcycles in Kenya's road traffic had initially evoked a negative stereotype reminiscent of a childhood conversation with my father. But in this memorable episode I became aware of a positive practical affordance that left me with a more humane interpretation.

The final essay, **Helping a traveler find his way,** describes an illuminating experience in Philadelphia in 2019 that highlighted for me how much my global wanderings over the years had depended on hospitality by strangers. In unpretentious empathy with a person who is evidently out of his depth due to his unfamiliarity with the affordances of the place and associated local practices, time and again strangers courteously explained a way forward on my journey as a matter of common decency – a virtue essential to peaceful coexistence that carries weight in times of crisis such as Europe faced in the Holocaust and many societies face today.

Scattered across these essays are oblique invocations of my preoccupations with aesthetic sensitivity and linguistic versatility, grounded in the humanistic tradition of the humanities that tend to contrast with the canons of positivist natural science. I hope they illustrate for readers how those competing research paradigms can complement one another in the emerging field of cultural developmental psychology.

RS

Lusaka: June 2025

Godparenthood

John Dawe was the first friend I made at Corpus Christi college, Oxford, where we were both admitted in the same year, 1962. He came from a high school in Cornwall, aspiring for a degree in English, I from a gap year between completing my high school at Westminster and "coming up" to Oxford, during which I had been enrolled as a "non-graduating student" at the University of Singapore. My high school studies had been centred on "the classics", i.e. ancient Greek and Latin language, literature, history and philosophy; in Singapore I had focused mainly on English literature, but had decided to register at Oxford for a multidisciplinary degree programme in Psychology and Philosophy.

We bonded over admiration of the English poetry of the Romantics, especially Keats and Shelley, and we also sensed that we were each emotionally embedded in an adult romantic relationship.

John's partner was Wendy, a little older than him and employed as a schoolteacher outside the university. Mine was Esther, also a few years older than me, recently arrived from Singapore and dividing her time in London between looking for work as a teacher and helping with domestic care for the newborn baby of her sister who was holding down a full-time job.

As freshmen we were both required by Corpus to reside in bachelor quarters on the premises of the college and to attend most evening meals in the refectory. Both of us were quite mystified by the rituals of college dinners, and were irritated by the rigidity of the time limit for checking in to college at night. As soon as regulations would permit, we each intended to find accommodation outside college, where we would be able to schedule our own feeding and sleeping arrangements as independent adults – including, of course, spending the night with our respective partner.

Our friendship grew unselfconsciously out of conversations about our romantic relationships and shared generational aspirations for societal acceptance as adults (we were both 18). We chatted informally in each other's college rooms, student lounges, local pubs, and occasionally in student gatherings linked to amateur drama. John and his friend Roger, also at Corpus, had been high school classmates in Cornwall, where they enjoyed acting in school productions at the Minack Theatre, a spectacular outdoor theatre on the coast near Land's End.

Their descriptions of the cliffside setting looking out over the sea were almost as inspiring as my first visit there some years later. I too had enjoyed acting at Westminster in school productions of Strindberg's *Easter* and Terence's *Adelphi*. Unlike John and Roger, my degree programme at Oxford did not include any study of literature. But a significant part of my spirit (mental life) continued to relish reading poetry and novels, watching theatrical plays and cinema. I even auditioned successfully for the leading role in two student productions: *Caligula* (by Camus 1944) and *The Revenger's Tragedy* (by Tourneur 1607).

I don't recall ever explicitly discussing philosophy with John. But, as is common between friends, we shared ideas about religion. We had both been exposed to the Church of England and read much of the Bible, but neither of us was a regular, churchgoing Christian, whereas both of our romantic partners were more conventionally devout, regular participants in church services, Wendy as a protestant, Esther as a catholic. Our friendship included those diverse particularities in religious outlook as unproblematic: we knew that each of us and our respective partners had grown up in different sociocultural contexts, and took it for granted that we had different backgrounds, personal life-journeys and hence different affiliations with particular congregations, each of which was likely to subscribe to subtly different interpretations of the Christian faith. But we shared an intuitive conviction that our moral outlook on personal relationships was broadly similar.

During our first year at Oxford, John and Wendy decided to get married, and I attended their wedding in church. They moved into a rented flat in town, where I became a frequent visitor. And early in the second year I learned that they were expecting their first child. Soon after she was born, they invited me to become her godfather. I was honoured and delighted. I was glad to accept on the strength of our personal friendship. I told them that I had benefitted greatly in my own childhood from the nurturant kindness of my godfather Richard Hankey (a close friend of my father from their undergraduate college days together) and my godmother Ric Winkler (a close friend of my mother from their undergraduate college days together).

However, when John and his wife explained that they would like me to participate in their baby daughter's Christening ceremony in the College chapel, I found it a bit disconcerting since I had no interest in providing religious counselling or guidance to my god-daughter. The service format demanded that as godparent I affirm a commitment to supporting the moral and spiritual development of this child, and I wondered if it might not be hypocritical to do so. Neither Richard nor Ric were church-going Christians and we had never conversed about religion as far as I could remember. But they were both "there for me" in important ways as I was growing up, known to my parents and trusted by them, but also independently supportive of me a person.

I eventually resolved the conflict by phrasing my utterances in the service as performative in the sense of "doing things with words" (a la Austin). I told myself that I had clearly confided to my friends, the child's parents, that I did not subscribe to the full corpus of Christian faith, but that I was sincere in wanting to "be there" for Amanda as a trusted adult beyond her immediate family in the way that my godparents had been there for me at the request of my agnostic parents. Pronouncing my commitment in the language of the Church of England baptism liturgy was, I told myself, symbolically performative communication, signifying to Amanda's parents my personal commitment to a supportive, nurturant role in their daughter's life in years to come. My sincerity in making that commitment warranted for me that my participation in the ceremony was not hypocritical, but was a nuanced way of expressing the commitment in the language-game (a la Wittgenstein) of a cultural ritual we all understood in somewhat different ways but appreciated as way of solemnifying our group relationship.

For true-believers, deeply embedded in a tradition of religious practices, I suppose my Austinian performative interpretation of the vows that I pronounced that day would seem inadequate, if not blasphemous, and certainly in some sense insincere or hypocritical. But, looking back on our relationship as peers growing into adult citizenship of mid-twentieth century England, it seems to me that our under-defined, consensual construal of a shared moral compass was socio-culturally normal, at least among middle-class intellectuals. Most of the rituals practiced by the Church of England in that era included features that gave them an appearance of being old-fashioned. In the analysis of metaphors in the representation of explanatory theories, such features can be construed as "excess meaning»[3]. For instance, the enduring ritual of showering newlyweds with confetti derives from a metaphor of fertility that young couples in the era of scientific family planning with contraceptive intervention might find offensive, implying that the only (or most important) function of marriage is to bear children. And the metaphor proposed by Jesus in the biblical story of the last supper might be abhorrent to some 20th century English novices as connoting the drinking of blood. In that spirit, I would defend my performative utterance of phrases within the discourse of the Church of England liturgy as bracketing[4] my negative emotional reactions to some of the text as unbelievable "excess meaning" in order to focus on what all the participants agreed on as a valuable public endorsement of intentions for me to participate in a certain way in the protective nurturance of the focal child in years to come.

From a sociological perspective, my defence could be regarded as a symptom of the secularisation of English culture in the 20th century.

---

[3] Reese and Overton (1970, 120) define the "excess meaning" in a metaphor as "elements or relations that are only 'accidentally' present."

[4] The term bracketing is used in phenomenological methodology to connote separation of a concept or perception from the focal topic of reflection

How does that secular trend in Europe relate to the epistemological theory that emerged in Wittgenstein's later *Philosophical Investigations*, published posthumously (1958) under the editorial guidance of his student Anscombe? It was not until I studied Habermas' (1984) *Theory of communicative action*, long after leaving Oxford and parting ways with John Dawe as he migrated to Canada and I to Zambia, that I began to understand that Wittgenstein's notion of language games and Austin's notion of speech acts had ethical implications.

Habermas distinguished three types of "criticisable claim to validity" underpinning the possibility of rational communication: objective truth, normative appropriateness, and sincerity. Using that refined conceptualisation, I would now recast my defence against the charge of hypocrisy as follows. The principal goal of the social event in the college chapel was to affirm, in the presence of suitably authorised witnesses, my moral commitment to an agenda with respect to the future life-journey of Amanda. The ritual of the Church christening was understood by all participants as a way of generating an implicit contract between her parents and me as a godparent. By nominating me for that role they were declaring that they trusted me to act wisely in the interests of the growing person when and as her situation might require support over and above their own. And by proclaiming my commitment to providing such support, I was accepting their trust and promising to do my best to deserve it. The validity I claim for that speech act is not a matter of objective truth (let alone word-for-word adequacy of the liturgical text to capture the nature of my responsibilities), but rests on my understanding of the expectations Amanda's parents had of me as a godfather and on my conviction of the sincerity with which I intended to meet those expectations.

The 3 x 5 index card

The card on which the advert appeared was quite inconspicuous, one among many pinned on a corkboard in the hallway of the Psychology Department. But the text was an amazing combination of words I had never before seen gathered together in a single sentence: Research Perception Learning Children Zambia.

Research was a dominant preoccupation of my current intellectual life, as I wrestled with the write-up of my independent study project required for my graduation that month. Moreover, the relation of **perception** to **learning** by **children** was the theoretical focus of my study's inquiry, drawing on the publications of my Oxford mentors, Stuart Sutherland and Nick Mackintosh.

But **Zambia** belonged in a different compartment of my mind: a nation recently in the news for attaining independence from British colonial rule – a landmark event in the liberation of Southern Africa. The name of the new nation resonated in my imagination with the title of a popular book by its charismatic leader Kenneth Kaunda (KK)

"Zambia shall be free". My interest in decolonisation was quite passionate, grounded in personal engagement with the social agenda of resisting oppressive, discriminatory practices in Singapore and in England. I had witnessed with disgust the crude racist exclusion of immigrants and visiting students of colour on other 3x5 index cards advertising accommodation for rent with the mantra: "no children, no pets, no coloureds". More intriguingly, the word resonated with my ill-formed aspirations of solidarity with opposition to the institutionalised system of *apartheid* in South Africa. As a student activist, I was excited by Zambia's accession to independence as a sign of progress in the international campaign to deligitimise *apartheid*. My personal search to date for a satisfactory explanation of racial intolerance and how to reduce it had centered around the psychology of attitudes and prejudice. I was inspired by the scholarship of Henri Tajfel, and had sought out a series of tutorials with him, as well as advice on the design of a student survey of discrimination by Oxford landladies against international students of colour.

Children had featured marginally in both of those compartments of my thinking. In my research on perception and learning, children featured as representatives of the human species that seemed to me inexcusably absent from the studies of attention theory by my mentors Sutherland and Mackintosh. My study had been designed to fill that gap by exploring how attention mediated children's learning. Coincidentally, this had brought me into sustained interaction with young children for the first time in my life. A course assignment of unstructured observation earlier in the year had exposed me to the behaviour of young children enrolled in a local kindergarten, and I had returned to the facility to secure a site for my assignment of independent research. In that context, my visits had assumed a structured character that allowed me to collect data efficiently for my project. But this had left me dimly feeling regret at the lack of significant insight into the thoughts and feelings of those mysteriously charming little people. In the domain of international politics, children had featured as token representatives of oppression, silent victims of political injustice, photographed living in conditions of material poverty.

So, juxtaposition of the word **children** with **Zambia** on the one hand and on the other with **perception** and **learning** struck me as a provocative anomaly. What was this call for **research in Zambia on children's perception and learning** getting at? Did it have any relevance to my personal, open-ended search for job opportunities?

The text on the little card went on to offer some exciting encouragement. The advert stated that eligible candidates should hold a bachelor's degree in psychology, and that the conditions of employment for a successful applicant would include not only a salary, local accommodation and international travel every two years between Zambia and a doctoral degree-granting institution in the UK. It would also confer the status of Junior Research Fellow on the academic faculty of a brand-new university, in a newly created Human

Development Research Unit (HDRU). As I jotted down the details of how to apply, I began to imagine myself stepping into an adult phase of life, independent of my parents, poised to participate in the exhilaration of a society newly liberated from colonial oppression.

At that first encounter, my imagination was provoked to search for wisdom along a new pathway. The itinerary followed twists and turns over the next decade, bringing me into productive communication with Alastair Heron, author of that little text, who became my first boss; with Jan Deregowski, a friendly neighbour and collaborator, who schooled me in statistical analysis; with Stuart Sutherland, who introduced me to the radical epistemology of Chomsky; and later with Alastair Mundy-Castle and Mubanga Kashoki, who from their widely separated perspectives introduced me to the field of sociolinguistics. They opened me up to the writings of Dell Hymes, Fishman, Labov and Gumperz, inspiring me to undertake studies in Zambia and to join the intellectual community of the Zambia Language Group.

The terms of reference of the advert were informed by Heron's administrative creativity, making the case to the British government of the 1960s for a wisely open-ended allocation of funds, and leveraging his friendship with KK and other members of the incoming leadership of the Zambian government to accept them for staffing and infrastructure of the HDRU. The unit was dedicated to generation of a locally collected body of scientific knowledge that Heron argued was essential grounding for teaching about human development in the new nation's first ever university.

To call my application in response to the advert a "juncture" tends to oversimplify an extended process as a "trajectory" energised by the ballistic force of a single stimulus (Welford 1967). Yet, in reality, the course of my development was shaped by a series of interpretive decisions taken in co-constructive interaction with diverse other persons. Each with his or her complex repertoire of cognitions, motives and attitudes. Neither Heron nor the British government, nor indeed KK with his passionate commitment to the project of a national university, let alone Stuart Sutherland with his philosophical insight into the programmatic nature of transformational grammar, could have anticipated in 1965 that the defining experience of living in Zambia would eventually lead me to conclude that the development of children in this society is better interpreted in terms of a theory of *nzelu* than by an information-processing model of intelligence (Serpell 2000).

My decision to apply for (and later to accept) appointment as a researcher on the faculty of UNZA was in part motivated by my personal agenda of affirming my independent identity. The contract offered a practical opportunity to sustain economically a marital partnership with my chosen lover, Esther, in a social setting where our inter-racial relationship would be legally recognised as normal.

I surmised that we would likely find an equally receptive attitude by the political elite if I were to take a position in Botswana, where the incoming head of government was the controversial Seretse Khama. He had famously stood up for his own inter-racial marriage in the face of conservative attitudes both by traditional elders of the indigenous society and by hypocritical British politicians. The latter were intent on extricating Britain from its imperial obligations towards its Protectorate while maintaining cooperative relations with the apartheid regime in South Africa, a rich source of mineral wealth. The prospect of living in a nation poised to attain political sovereignty under the leadership of a man with such ostensible commitment to inter-racial harmony appealed to me even more than Zambia. I even went as far as interviewing for a position in the pioneering secondary school in Serowe managed by Patrick van Rensburg during his brief visit to London. But the duties he explained to me as my responsibility if I were to join the school as an (untrained) teacher of English seemed to me less professionally exciting than those laid out by Heron in correspondence about the position of a research fellow at UNZA.

My letter of application, as I recall, was phrased with idealistic commitment to the possibility of radical societal change. Looking back, I now recognise, thanks to Piaget, that my confidence reflected a characteristically adolescent belief in formal operational logic. Zambia was ostensibly embarking on an explicit programme of nation-building informed by the philosophical principle of equality between races in direct contradiction to the apartheid ideology of South Africa. I would consider it an honour to engage, albeit at a humble level, with promotion of that social agenda. My credentials included evidence of active engagement with a kindred political agenda of societal change in English society.

On the other hand, I declared a commitment to the principles of systematic scientific inquiry about the nature of human perception and learning. As evidence of my competence to conduct such research, I cited the degree awarded to me by Oxford University and my provisional acceptance by the University of Sussex as a doctoral student under the sponsorship of the distinguished scholar, Professor Sutherland. Looking back, I realise that the credibility of combining my self-advocacy as a prospective agent of progressive societal change with the credential of scholarly aptitude rested on unproblematised logic about how technical knowledge relates to communicative validity (Habermas). I was, without invoking either term, a positivist and a universalist. I had virtually no evidence that the particular theory of learning advanced by Sutherland was useful in understanding human development, let alone congruent with the beliefs and aspirations of the people of Zambia. But I had so completely appropriated the epistemological premise of the European renaissance Enlightenment, what Berlin has termed "the certainty of method", that I assumed the empirical methods of contemporary

Western science would guarantee generation of universally valid knowledge relevant to humans everywhere.

It took completion of a doctoral programme of research framed in those positivistic terms and disenchantment with the insights that it generated for me to open up my intellectual agenda to exploration of multiple, different ways of knowing. That reappraisal of my world view arose not just from encountering Alastair Mundy-Castle and Mubanga Kashoki, but also from the personal agenda of negotiating acceptance in Zambian society through my marital partnership with Namposya. The interpenetration of my research career arising from my response to that advert on a 3x5" index card and other dimensions of my personal life-journey is the subject of my 2024 book, *In search of integrity: a life-journey across diverse contexts*. The initial door opened for me by the advert prompted a juncture in my life-journey very different from the journeys of the other two early career scholars who responded to it at the same time and joined me in the HDRU as founding research fellows in 1965, Jan Deregowski and Donald Munro.

This is a nice house

At last I could let go of his hand, now that we had transitioned from the airport shuttle bus into a hotel. A porter wheeled our baggage into the lift, pressed the button for the 6th floor, and set out with his trolley along the corridor. Five-year-old Derek rushed ahead, peering through the railing at the brightly-lit atrium of the lobby below, and testing the plushy carpet under foot. Turning back to check on me, he exclaimed "This is a nice house, Papa. Can we stay here?"

I knew at once that he was not referring to our overnight stop-over covered by our tickets under the provisions of interline regulations. He was recalling my explanations of the impending trip as we packed up our household goods in Lusaka for removal to a new city, far way in England, called Manchester. We would be living there for a change, I told him, while Papa starts a new job and you start at a new school. As soon as we got to England, we would start looking for a house to live in – where he would have his own room with his own bed to sleep in and keep all his toys and books. There would also be a kitchen and a sitting room just like our house in Lusaka.

It was the newly opened Hilton Hotel, a glossy, prestigious building in the centre of Nairobi where I had been delighted to learn from the airline information desk we would be accommodated for the night. The next morning, we would return to the airport to catch a flight on the next leg of our journey to Lagos, where we would connect with a flight to Kano, for a week-long visit to our friends the Rayans before finally proceeding to London, where we would catch a train to Manchester. "No, Derek - this is a lovely hotel, isn't it? But we are only staying here for one night!" I replied, hoping that would be enough explanation for now.

It was the first of a series of challenging questions addressed to me as we negotiated a way forward in our life together as father and son, from Zambian to English society. Before finding a house to make our home in Manchester, we were kindly welcomed as guests in the family of a student friend of my new boss, Peter Mittler, Director of the research centre where I would be working. I don't remember her name or whether she had children of her own. She was excited by the opportunity to welcome us as visitors from a Third World country, and eager to help with selecting a day care facility where Derek would be in a safe and nurturant niche while his single parent was busy at work, until such time as the boy was admitted to a suitable kindergarten. I am most grateful to her for welcoming us so warmly, and especially for introducing me to a fellow spirit, Morgan Morison, who became a long-term friend.

Morgan and I quickly bonded, intuitively appreciating one another's personal commitment to intimate inter-racial relationships. His complexion announced a biological heritage of mixed African and European descent, while that of his wife Shirley was pinko-grey like mine. And their boys displayed a mixture of the two strands that resonated for me with Derek's facial display of European and Asian traits. Grounded in that sense of commonality as citizens of the world, we explored political issues confronting English society and discovered a shared commitment to promoting tolerance among people of diverse ethnic and cultural origins for the benefit of the emerging next generation that included our children. His sons and Derek soon became friendly playmates.

The worst disappointment I witnessed in that period of transition was when I left Derek in the care of a team of well-meaning, professional caregiving staff at a daycare centre, which was devoid of any familiar, trustworthy adults. His tears at the moment of separation were hard to bear as I took off to attend to necessary tasks. And yet, when I returned a few hours later to pick him up, disconcertingly but convincingly, I was assured by the staff that he had stopped crying within a few minutes and gone on to spend a cheerfully companionable day interacting confidently with the other children.

The 'nice house' that we eventually secured on rent in a safe and accessible neighbourhood included the essential room of his own to keep his toys and books, and a back garden that opened onto a playing field where we played football together. But the encompassing middle-class, suburban neighbourhood was disapproving of my colourful flood of overnight guests and my neglect of the front lawn. So our lease was not renewed at the end of the year, and we had to move again.

Derek's choice of words that day as he expressed his admiration of the Nairobi Hilton was a delightful example of how a person deploys their existing vocabulary to embrace a novel experience - forcing a new phenomenon into the investigator's conceptual box, as Thomas Kuhn tells us that scientific theorists do. Years later, in 2002, a young Malawian student traveling with me on our way to a rural fieldsite for research on child development, was sharing opinions with me about the music on cassettes that we played on the car's tape-deck. Earlier she had helped me to select a tape by the Zimbabwean pop icon Oliver Mtukudzi to purchase from a street vendor at the station where we stopped to buy gas. He was one of her favourite artists, famous in the region, but I had never heard of him before. Now it was my turn to introduce her to one of my favourite Beethoven concertos. When the orchestra paused at the end of the first movement, she exclaimed "You mean that was all one song ?!"

But over and above expressing admiration for a new experience, Derek was sending me a timely reminder of our preparatory discussion of what our journey would be about, and signalling that from his perspective its most important goal was to settle into a new place that would qualify as our family home.

The slice of pizza

We were in a follow-up phase of our wedding celebrations. A month or two after the elaborate multi-cultural sequence of events in Lusaka in March 1973.

Rather than flying out my mother and father to Lusaka, they had invited us to meet up with them in England, where we dressed up in our fancy outfits for photographs: Namposya resplendent in her home-made, white wedding dress posing with me in my tailored lounge suit and each of her new parents-in-law, to record for Namposya's family of origin back home, and for posterity, the blessing of our union by the Serpell family in England. Derek, my seven-year-old son from my previous marriage, after greeting his beloved English grandparents and sharing with us some sumptuous hotel meals, had now gone to spend time with his mother, leaving the two of us newly-weds to have a second honeymoon in UK. Like the wedding in Zambia in March, this honeymoon came as a refreshingly private outing in the wake of a vibrant social gathering. But it was somewhat under-financed due to extravagant expenditures on the social events.

We had travelled to Manchester to attend, as a special treat, a concert by the magnificent international star, Nana Mouskouri, performed at an upmarket theatre, and had purchased our expensive tickets at the door. Now there was an hour of down time before the event. We suddenly realised that we were both quite hungry, having eaten nothing since breakfast. Checking in our respective purses, we discovered that we had just enough between us to buy a light evening meal. So, we looked around for a modest restaurant. Those were the days before credit cards and ATMs became commonplace in Zambia. So, our dinner would have to be paid for in cash, and we needed to reserve some for the bus-ride to our lodging for the night.

The pizza joint we found within the vicinity of the theatre was brightly lit and giving out an appetising fragrance. We sat down and eagerly inspected the menu. It turned out that what we could afford was just a single slice of pizza. So we laughed and agreed to share just that, to keep our tummies from rumbling through the concert. For both of us the challenge immediately brought to mind the counsel we had received a few weeks earlier from Namposya's two elderly aunties, sitting on the floor of my Lusaka house.

They had come to the house to check up on our consummation of the marriage, early in the morning after the wedding ceremonies. I was a bit unprepared for this particular event, having assumed that we were now released as a couple for some privacy, away from the intense gaze of the many elders gathered at the public venue. But Namposya urged me to invite the two ladies in, and they installed themselves in the sitting room. They had brought with them an *imbaula* (charcoal brazier), which they proceeded to light, inviting us to sit on the floor facing them. When the coals had turned to white hot embers, one of them placed a slab of tin on the top and started to explain in ciMambwe what this was all about. The message, that Namposya translated concurrently, unfolded as follows:

> "Yesterday, in front of the whole family and all the invited guests, you two took a vow to enter into a partnership of love for the rest of your lives. You promised to be true to each other and to share the responsibility of raising your future children together. This ceremony with the *imbaula* is to explain to you the importance of sharing. Suppose, one day, your family falls on hard times: you are so poor that the only food left in your larder is this one nut."

She held up a single groundnut and placed it on the tin plate.

> "Because you are now partners in marriage, you must be willing to share what little you have. When the nut is cooked, you must divide it between you, half each."

Lifting the roasted nut in her gnarled fingers, the old lady broke it in two and offered one half to each of us to eat. And, of course, we complied.

41

Now, as we divided our one slice of pizza, we recalled the ceremony of the nut, and agreed that this was an occasion to put into practice our great-aunties' grandparental wisdom. Small though it was, the pizza was a delicious opportunity to practice the philosophical commitment to sharing we had made in our marriage vows. Over the years, we recalled this little incident in Manchester in a miniature re-enactment of the lesson conveyed to us in Lusaka in 1973.

Our status in the extended network of family gradually evolved from a pair of neophytes to an established couple endowed with wisdom accumulated from experience. As such, we were approached from time to time by a younger member of the family with a request to offer counsel to a couple embarking on marriage, or to a married couple whose union was experiencing a problem. Often the request was channelled through an elder of the family, invoking as a rationale that our particular union seemed to be flourishing.

Namposya built on our first attempt to convey to a young couple what we had learned from the ceremony of the nut, which we re-enacted for them with an *imbaula*. We further explained with a recollection of the slice of pizza, that had convinced us of the relevance of the Mambwe maxim of sharing to our own lives in the contemporary world. In the title of her unpublished autobiography, Namposya named it "The Bonding Ceremony".

Jive talk

We were gathered around the table for a weekend family lunch outing, in a cafeteria of the University of Hawaii. Sighting us from afar, a lively, laughing man introduced himself:

> "Hello, how are you? My name is Olatunde. I'm from Nigeria. And where are you people from? From Africa, I'm sure ! But from which country?"

I supposed it was the embroidered collar of my shirt that gave us away, or was it the multiple shades of our complexions – a chocolate brown motherly woman, caramel and beige children?

> "We are from Zambia," I explained, "visiting Hawaii where I am working at the East-West Centre … Are you a lecturer here at the University, or a student? From your name I guess you are maybe Nigerian?"

> "No, man. I am a student. Yes, from Nigeria. But I have been here a long time. So welcome! I am so glad to meet you from Zambia, the country of KK! When did you come to Hawaii?"

Namposya introduced herself and the children, 10-year-old Derek, 3-year-old Zewe and baby Chisha. We soon established that we were newcomers to Honolulu, short-term sojourners, while he was an established resident, excited to meet up with some Africans, as there were so few Africans in Hawaii. He was enthusiastic about extending hospitality to us as members of a fictive community of *real* Africans, kinspeople of his own family as distinct from the self-styled African-Americans - many of whom were among his friends and fellow-students on campus.

> "You must come to my home and meet my wife – I live not far from here. Where are you staying?"

I explained that we were living in a rented apartment the other side of town, and would be returning there shortly as the kids and I would need to settle down for the night in readiness for tomorrow's routines of school and work.

> "No, no!" he exclaimed – "first you must visit my home and meet the family. Your wife must meet my wife, and your kids meet my kids. Even if it's just a short visit – so that you know where we stay."

We agreed on condition that we could get away soon after sunset, and strategized how best to drive in his car and ours the short distance from campus to his home. We should just follow him, and he would drive slowly so that we didn't lose sight of his car in the traffic. No other directions were given nor an address of our destination.

Downstairs in the car park, I pulled up in our compact, second-hand Toyota behind his big, somewhat battered, black American sedan and waited for him to pull out into the traffic. As soon as possible, I followed him into the middle lane, while the children chatted excitedly on the back seat about the prospect of meeting another African family. Quite abruptly, the car we were following turned into the left lane and entered an intersection, making a U-turn into the traffic on the other side of the dual carriageway. "He's turning, Papa" came the warning from my attentive passengers "you need to make a U-turn!" But I could see a traffic sign clearly prohibiting U-turns at that intersection. " I can't," I said "it's not allowed". "But if you don't turn here, we'll never keep track of them: the next U-turn is miles away along this road …" Time for a quick decision. There was little traffic at this time of day, and they were right, we might well lose track of our welcoming guide if we continued on this road. I checked my rear-mirror and swung into the intersection, following closely the route taken by the other car.

I had barely straightened the steering wheel when I heard the strident whine of a police siren. A motor-cycle traffic cop had seen our illegal manoeuvre and was pointing us to pull over to the side of the road. The two cars pulled up next to each other, and the two drivers, Olatunde and I, stepped out to confront the officer, who had parked his motorbike and was holding a clip board and pen, poised to record the incident. He had tipped back his helmet revealing a Chinese face.

"Y'all know what you just did: no U-turns are allowed back there. That's an offence!"

Olatunde and I started simultaneously to explain.

"I'm sorry, officer, I am new to Hawaii. I didn't know U-turns are forbidden at that junction, "I lied. "This is my first time to drive in this part of town, and was just following my new friend here, who is directing me to his home."

"No, no, no," exclaimed Olatunde. "It's my mistake, Officer. This gentleman is new to Hawaii. He was just following my example. I committed the offence of making a U-turn. Please don't charge him. Charge me!"

"But he was just trying to assist me," I protested. "Please excuse him, Officer. It's really my fault. I'm sure he just forgot about the regulation, while he was trying to help me, a stranger in this city..."

The policeman held up his hand to silence us, and demanded to see our documents. We both produced car registration and driving licenses. After scrutinising them, he looked at me and asked "you don't have an American license?" "No, sir. I am just here in Hawaii for four months. And I was told I can drive here on my Zambian license for this short stay." Turning to Olatunde, he asked "So you are from Zambia?"

"No, no, Officer. I am an established resident here. As you can see, I have an American license, issued here in Honolulu".

"So, what is your excuse for making an illegal U-turn?"

"Well, you see, this gentleman and his family are new here in Hawaii. And I want to show them where I live, to welcome them as visitors to Hawaii. So I told him to follow me in his car. I live just nearby. But I figured if I took the long road, he might lose track of me. And, really there is hardly any traffic on a Sunday evening. So I thought maybe I should make the U-turn here, and he could follow me. Please excuse my mistake, Officer. Just this one time, since there wasn't any disturbance of the traffic. You could exercise some lenience. I promise I won't make that mistake again."

The policeman looked through the window of my car and saw my wife and children, one of whom had a Chinese-European physiognomy of the type widely represented in the local population. "Are these your family?" he asked. "Yes, Sir, that is my wife and those are my children". Hesitantly, he handed me back my green Zambian driving license - a little booklet quite unlike an American license, but containing a clearly recognisable portrait photo of me – a white man… Then he turned to Olatunde and said "so you are a resident of Hawaii? You should know better than to make a U-turn here. There are signs to show it's prohibited. But how come it's him, and not you, driving on an African license?"

Giving Olatunde back his license, he shrugged and exclaimed "You guys are giving me some jive talk!" He mounted his motorbike and drove off.

What kind of nuts?

It started as an outing to share with Namposya what I had been learning while she was busy in her course for professionals in international finance. Her four-month sojourn in Washington DC was sponsored by the International Monetary Fund (the IMF). And the Fund had generously agreed to pay my fare from Lusaka, so that I could stay with her in their apartment on Dupont Circle. Most of Namposya's daytime hours were taken up with her studies. So I took the opportunity to enrol in a beginner's course on American Sign Language (ASL) at Gallaudet University. The Institution was established in the 19th century in the name of the pioneering educator Thomas Gallaudet who, together with a deaf Frenchman Laurent Clerc, brought the French sign language to America.

My first introduction to that bit of history had been Harlan Lane's brilliant narrative book, *The Wild Boy of Aveyron* (1976), purchased during my first visit to the United States, after hearing the author speak about it in a guest lecture at Rockefeller University. I had given little thought to the disputatious history of education for the deaf during my sojourn in Manchester, where my research had focused on education for children with severe learning disability. But my interest had been revived by collaborative preparation for the International Year of Disabled Persons (IYDP – 1981) with a deaf teacher who became a personal friend, Mackenzie Mbewe. I was beginning to learn from him and from his network of deaf friends and acquaintances about the isolation they experienced from the mainstream of Zambian society. From my classes at Gallaudet, I was becoming aware that ASL was undergoing a transformational change in status, from an obscure, specialised pedagogical resource to a flourishing cultural medium for public performance of drama and even composition of poetry. Yet it was still subject to resistance by some authorities in the field of special education, who argued that using ASL as a medium of instruction for deaf children was a dysfunctional distraction from the agenda of empowering students with the ability to communicate with 'normal' persons with speech.

I was intrigued by the opportunity to acquire some competence in ASL, a language claimed by growing numbers of deaf persons in America as their natural first language, intrinsically suited to their everyday needs, generative of a distinctive culture in which they could take pride. Other students in the class introduced themselves as either hearing parents of a deaf child or professional providers of public services, such as the Post Office. Each of them explained with enthusiasm their personal motivation for learning how to communicate in ASL with their own deaf child or with deaf customers at work. By comparison, I had felt a bit embarrassed to admit that my motivation was primarily theoretical and that I was unlikely, as a short-term sojourner in the US, to have much opportunity to put what I was learning into practice. Nevertheless, I found the instructor's nuanced presentation of the language and its everyday uses illuminating.

Today I was excited by the opportunity to explore with Namposya what student life was like on the Gallaudet campus. Someone in my class had mentioned that there would be a major social event in the form of a concert in the big hall, where electronic music would be played at the high volume that profoundly deaf people appreciate, with vibrations strong enough to detect with their feet through the floor. Bracing ourselves to endure what for us was a deafening assault on our ears, Namposya and I made our way into the hall and watched with admiration as couples and singles threw themselves with abandon into energetically coordinated dance.

In the back of my mind, I began to worry about the journey home. In the course of my trips across the city between Dupont Circle and Gallaudet, I had learned that the Metro Bus system required each passenger to deposit an exact change amount into the automated fare box which did not accept bank notes. Earlier that day, after paying for our trip, we had discovered that we had no more coins between us – only 20-dollar notes. We needed, before boarding a bus to go home, to exchange one of our notes for some coins. I left Namposya to wait while I went to the bar in search of change.

The barman was very busy serving thirsty customers with drinks. Catching his eye was quite a challenge. Holding out a twenty-dollar note, I mouthed a request for two cokes. He read my lips correctly and handed me two bottles and some smaller denomination notes. Inwardly cursing my poor calculations, I shook my head, handed him back a ten-dollar note, and asked him for some nuts. Surely that would force him to give me some small change in coins? At first, he frowned, not understanding my request. So, I pointed at the packets of nuts on display and held up my hand to finger-spell N_U_T_S. My teacher had assured me that, while it was not standard ASL practice to use finger-spelling for common words like nuts, every literate ASL speaker was familiar with the manual signs for letters of the alphabet, since they are used to dictate unfamiliar words like a new person's name. Quick as a flash, the barman responded orally "What kind of nuts?"

Too late, I realised I had found my way into a trap. What I wanted was nuts cheap enough that the correct change would be only payable in coins. But I had no idea of the different prices of the varieties of nuts on display. Moreover, I was struggling to remember the handshapes required to finger-spell each letter. I needed to respond quickly enough to hold his attention before he turned away to serve another of the bustling customers all around me holding out money to get next in line. In desperation I formed the letter C, and before I could change my mind, he handed me a pack of cashew nuts (the most expensive variety on display!) and a five-dollar note.

I could see I had exhausted the patience of both the barman and his enervated crowd of customers. Folornly, I carried away my unwanted bottles of drink and packet of nuts, wending my way through the exuberant masses on the dance floor. As a last resort, I tried writing on a scrap of paper "PLEASE CAN YOU HELP ME WITH SOME SMALL CHANGE FOR THE BUS?" and held it up, together with the five-dollar note, in the face of several dancers on the floor. Some turned away without reading it, others shook their head, and I soon gave up. For the first time in my life, I felt genuinely frustrated and hurt by exclusion on the basis of being marginal: I didn't belong here. By my own doing, due to my incompetence, I was radically out of place.

I rejoined Namposya and we escaped from the blaring music into the quiet, darkening grounds of the campus, down the hill to the main gate, out onto the sidewalk of the busy city street. We hurried past the first bus stop, along a dark, deserted pavement in search of hearing help, and eventually found a bottle store where the salesperson kindly agreed to exchange the note for coins. Then we boarded a bus and safely reached home.

My first-hand experience of exclusion prompted me to look afresh at the ongoing debate between advocates of oral education (supported with lip-reading and hearing-aids) and promoters of sign language as an instrument of social solidarity among deaf persons. What had previously seemed a theoretically plausible argument by proponents of sign now impressed me as evidence of a cultural resource with unique affordances for personal development essential for a deaf person, situated in a predominantly hearing world, to feel confident of his or her rights as a citizen to participate in normal social intercourse.

Graffiti

My son Derek was 17 when the rest of our nuclear family moved to Hull for a year. I was on sabbatical leave from UNZA, based at the University of Hull as a visiting professor in the Psychology Department, and we had been allocated a comfortable, small town-house on Cottingham Road. Namposya was enrolled in an MSc programme in Economics, and the girls (aged 3, 7, 9, and 16) were enrolled in various educational programmes around the city.

As we settled in, we soon learned about Hull's world-renowned historical luminary, William Wilberforce, pioneer of the abolitionist movement in Britain in the late 18th century and local Member of Parliament. The movement had culminated in the Parliamentary Act of 1807 that abolished the British slave trade, followed by the Slavery Abolition Act of 1833, the year in which Wilberforce died. His house was a national monument and museum, and we visited it *en famille*, bringing home as a souvenir a child-friendly facsimile of an 18th century abolitionist pamphlet's illustration of a slave ship densely packed with its human cargo. The girls were welcomed into Hull's public schools as African visitors with proud rhetorical allusions to the city's history as home of an iconic pioneer of the movement to restore freedom and dignity to the peoples of Africa.

Derek, by this phase in his life-journey, had re-located from Lusaka to live with his mother in Lichfield, the other side of England – across the pennines, near Birmingham. He came to Hull for a summer holiday, rejoining the family he had grown up in, and affording me an extended opportunity to renew our bond as father and son.

One morning on a walk around town, we were surprised to come across some garish graffiti, spray-painted on a wall facing us as we stepped off the zebra crossing over a busy main street in the city centre. The words were grossly insulting, addressed to persons of colour in the slang of current racist slogans -known to Derek from the streets of Birmingham and to me from TV coverage of the wave of social unrest in England manifested in the 1981 city riots in London, Liverpool and Birmingham. I was shocked to see such vile hate speech displayed in public in the proudly anti-racist city of Hull.

Back at the house, we told Namposya, out of earshot of the young girls, what we had seen. She agreed with me that it was strikingly out of character with the predominant culture of Hull as we had come to know it during our sojourn there in the past several months. Namposya attested that she had encountered no such explicit expressions of hostility, either on the campus or in the local shopping malls. And we recalled the inclusive warmth with which our girls had been welcomed by their various school teachers and classmates, several of whom had invited them into their homes for birthday parties.

I was, of course, not a long-term resident and at the age of 39 had long given up on the myth of England as a colour-blind, egalitarian society, favouring a more 'salad-bowl' metaphor and negotiated consensus-building among diverse, mutually respectful ethnocultural groups. But, over the course of our comfortably accepted family sojourn in Hull, I had developed a cautious sense of local belonging and, I now realised, a wishful pride in the dignity of the city's culture that I wanted to defend against this rough intrusion of alien intolerance.

As we mulled over it, I began to wonder how we as individuals should push back. Presumably, in due course the city's public works department would erase the offensive graffiti as part of routine maintenance. But it seemed unlikely that this would be done in the near future. Meanwhile, I felt it was outrageous that children of colour, including my own, resident in this generally inclusive urban community should be exposed to such aggressive hostile speech in a public space. Should we register a formal complaint? What would likely be the response? Would we not incur disapproval for demanding attention to a relatively minor issue, perhaps appearing to be thin-skinned, selfishly demanding priority for a matter that mainly affected us as a minority?

Rather than trying to enlist support from local colleagues, I decided to take responsibility myself for silencing this disgraceful outburst of hate speech. I invited Derek to join me, and he gladly agreed. We bought some cans of spray paint at a local shop, waited till the night was dark and made our way down town to revisit the site. The street was deserted. No sign of police patrols. Side by side, we set about spraying the wall, targeting each word until it was completely blotted out. Then, after admiring each other's work, we walked back home together, proud of our little achievement and happily bonding in excited celebration of our joint endeavour in a just cause.

My first draft of this essay was entitled "Good people break bad laws," inspired by a placard I had seen in a recent newscast, held up by a rioting protester to confront the police deployed to restore public order. But when I googled the phrase, I found it was borrowed from a book about the virtues of civil disobedience. Now it may be that, had we been interrupted that night by a local police officer, he or she would have told us we were violating some ordinance, taking the law into our own hands without authorisation. But, as I look back on the event, I am glad we took action, and that the escapade afforded us an opportunity to bond in moral conviction. I wanted to show my adolescent son, empathising with his disgust with racism, that it's ok to break the letter of the law if in doing so you're serving a good cause.

During my own late adolescence, I listened in awe to distinguished speakers in Trafalgar Square, addressing members of the Anti-

Apartheid movement, praising the protesters who burned their passes at Sharpeville, and calling on the British Parliament to enact a law banning racist hate speech. But even more than the AA marches, I remember with satisfaction the furtive act of intimidating my Headmaster with a fraudulent phone call posing as a journalist, that may have saved another young schoolboy from enduring the pain and humiliation of a violent caning.

In 2024 I had the unexpected pleasure of reading a new novel by one of my close family friends, Iris Mwanza, and realising that she had hit on another powerful strategy for pushing back against injustice, here in our beloved country of Zambia. Her fictional, but realistic, account of the misfortunes of Bessy in *The Lion's Den* is likely to be subtly effective in pushing back against demonising rhetoric, and to reduce interpersonal violence and social stigma against gay men. Of course, the heroine of the novel, like the author, will advocate openly for decriminalisation of consensual homosexual relations. But resistance is likely to take the form, as it did in England before the enactment of new laws in the 1960s, of hate speech liable to incite violence against individuals' basic human rights.

The pot of gold

We were driving in the family car, loudly debating how long it would take to reach our destination – Cape Maclear (site of the first Livingstonia Mission at the Southern end of Lake Malawi) where we could check in to a lodge for the night. This was a real family holiday, tacked on to the end of a business trip for Papa in Zomba, where the University of Malawi had engaged him as External Examiner for the Psychology Department. Our travel guidance had warned that the road to the lodge was unpaved, winding and rugged, and we were all feeling it, as the car bumped us around. Looking out of the windows all we could see was wild miombo woodland, scraggly trunks flitting by between brown grass and green treetops. But soon, I announced, we should be able to catch a glimpse of the lake, just around sunset. We turned a bend, mounted a steep slope and suddenly the view ahead of us opened up.

The sun was a brilliant ball of fire, poised over some island hills in the middle of a vast expanse of shimmering water. We stopped the car and clambered out to watch in awe as the ball slowly sank from a kaleidoscopic sky into the molten gold of the lake. "The pot of gold" I exclaimed, invoking the myth of 'where the rainbow ends'. Five-year-old Carla, the youngest of us, recognised the allusion, and her big sisters Chisha (aged ten) and Zewe (aged twelve) were happy to share the mystery as an elaboration of our family fantasy world, as was their mother Namposya.

After sunset that evening, we reached the lodge and, after a feast of lake fish and chips, the children soon dropped off to sleep under mosquito nets in a thatched rondavel, leaving us parents to relax. We walked down to the lakeshore, where we spread a chitenge on the beach, lay down together and made love in the dark, listening to the voices of local fishermen calling out to one another from their canoes, seeming just a few yards away. In the morning, we all swam in the lake, peered at the otters in their cave, and soon embarked on the next stage of our journey, crossing the border between Lilongwe and Chipata and traveling 600km along the Great East Road back to our home in Lusaka.

There were many other sights and events on that trip to talk about (elephants and mountains and people we met along the way). But a uniquely vivid recollection was the pot of gold. One day, soon after we got home, I laid out paints, brushes and paper in the porch of our family home, and invited the girls to each make a picture of it. Zewe's painting captures the psychedelic quality of the colours in the lake and the sky. Carla's painting highlights the motif of the sun setting on the water. And Chisha's painting dramatically centres on the sun's gold reflected in the lake. Their complementary visions of the shared event warm my heart with a treasured memory of how our family came together to relish and celebrate the beauty of nature.

CHISHA'S PAINTING

CARLA'S PAINTING

The art of painting was introduced to me as a child by my father, Michael, as a way of looking at the world through another person's eyes. He delighted in pointing out details of the artist's world in a time and place alien to us, and the stylistic nuances of how the artist portrayed it, nurturing in me a lifelong fascination with art as a way of representing and interpreting reality. My aesthetic appreciation of painting (and indeed of music) has remained a significant strand of my mental life, and I have sought to share it with others when opportunities arise. I do not think of myself as an artist in either domain but I find satisfaction both in the immediate impact of a painting and in understanding the history of its creation, interpretations of the artist's intentions, reflections on the social, cultural and historical context in which it was created and what the process and product tell us about human meaning-making.

ZEWE'S PAINTING

Gombrich[5] famously said that the secret of visual art is making comparisons that work. The search for what we now call photographic realism informed a programmatic endeavour within the culture of Western art culminating in the Renaissance application of the geometric laws of perspective. But there is more to "what works" in visual art than fidelity of representation on a two-dimensional surface of the visual array that is projected to the naked eye from a particular point in space. And, once the camera had been invented, such fidelity lost its appeal to Western artists, who started exploring comparisons at

---

[5] 1950. The story of Art

a less concrete level of equivalence, giving rise to the schools of impressionism, expressionism, cubism, etc.

A sizable body of research has been devoted to exploring what factors enter into the greater success of some pictures in evoking a particular object in the mind of the observer. It seems evident to me that artistic creation does more than surprise us with novelty. But I am still at a loss for words to capture the subjective experience of great beauty generated by the imaginative portrayal by another person of part of the world that we all share. What was the nature of that 'coup de foudre' that struck us individually and as a family with awe as we gazed out at the sunset over Lake Malawi that day? And what is the nature of the pleasure we share revisiting the three young artists' portrayal of that event?

Les signares

The first time I saw them it was the sway of their long robes that caught my attention – a burst of motion as they clustered energetically, in a corner of the hotel dining room, affirming their right to be there. Luckily for me, there was a vacant table where I could study them without distraction while I ate my breakfast.

I had already developed a fondness for the *boubou* style of dress worn by many of the women in Dakar and was planning to buy one or two for Namposya, to add to her Lusaka wardrobe. It already boasted a number of them in colourful tie-and-dye fabric, that I had purchased in Cote d'Ivoire on another conference trip. As I soaked up the ambience of the painting, I became entranced by the vibrant interaction among these tall, elegant women, seemingly in a marketplace, or gathering for some festive occasion. How many were they? And who was this pale-faced one?

It was a fancy hotel in Dakar, where I been accommodated by the organisers of an international conference. The next morning, I was delighted to find the same table available. So, I revisited them with a growing affection, relishing the flashes of colour on one woman's blouse and another bright flash in the folds of her dress, and yet another streaking from shoulder to knee height in the flow of light cotton that could have been the dress of the pale-faced woman or of someone else standing just behind her. Crowning these graceful figures were flourishes of colourful head-dresses bending in harmony with the women's bodies as if they were dancing.

On my third morning someone else had bagged my table before I arrived and I reluctantly sat elsewhere for my breakfast. But before leaving I walked over to give the painting one more glance. On an impulse I asked a waiter if by any chance any of the paintings on display were up for sale. "Mais oui Monsieur. Est-ce que vous desirez en acheter une ?" I pointed out my ladies and asked about the price. He explained that the price could only be quoted by the artist and he could arrange for me to meet this one's author later in the week.

It was on my last day in Dakar that I was introduced to Die Fall. She was dressed in a simple, traditional outfit – nothing as glamorous as the ladies in the painting. Yes, she was the artist. I asked about the topic and she confirmed that it was a market scene. "Et cette femme-là – est-ce que c'est une Europeene ?" Well, she retorted calmly, is that how you see her? I shyly observed that she had a pale complexion. The title of the painting, she told me, was "Les Signares" – a tip, if I had been less ignorant, as to why the woman's face was pale.

"LES SIGNARES" BY DIE FALL

After a small negotiation we settled on a price that was well above the total amount of local cash I had in hand. So, I drew some extra funds with my credit card from the hotel's ATM, took a photograph on my phone of the artist standing beside her masterpiece, and proudly left carrying the painting away with me. The airline staff agreed with me that the work of art could not be safely consigned to the hold and found a place for it behind the last row of passenger seats. And that is how "Les Signares" travelled from the hotel dining-room in Dakar to my Lusaka home.

It was only after I had installed it on a wall of my sitting-room room that I began to follow up the title of Die Fall's painting. Thanks to the internet, I soon discovered that *les signares* were a famous feature of Senegal's history, widely touted by the nation's tourism industry: an elite class of women of mixed descent born of sexual intercourse between European slavers and indigenous African women. Somehow this dramatic topic had escaped my notice during the trip I had made in Dakar to their ecosocial niche of Gore Island, accompanied by my new friend Kofi Marfo. We had divided our morning on the island between sharing ideas and experiences with graduate education for African scholars of child between development, and shopping for souvenir knick-knacks and colourful garments to take home for our respective wives and daughters. Eventually, in the middle of the day, we turned our attention to the conspicuous display on the ocean's edge of a stark reminder of the African continent's ghastly encounter with an earlier generation of visitors: the ruins of the fortress and dungeons that housed the notorious embarkation point for the trans-Atlantic slave trade.

We listened to the local guide's uncompromising account of the gruesome details of *La Maison des Esclaves,* gazing into the dark cells where captured men and women had been crammed in their hundreds and thousands over the course of three centuries, before being herded in shackles through the *Door of No Return* into ships that transported them to the Americas for sale as slaves, condemned to conditions of appalling cruelty to labour for the burgeoning economies of the European colonies. Despite the thrill of our shopping and the dazzling beauty of the coastal scenery, we were both stunned by the numbers and the stark simplicity of the buildings into a sombre mood that brought my normally exuberant friend to tears.

So, how did the grim history of enslavement relate to Die Fall's portrayal of those elegant black women of Senegal? The first image that came to my mind was of a rough Portuguese mariner-invader looking down through the grille, singling out amid a seething huddle of captives the voluptuous contours of a naked woman, commanding one of his minions to bring her to him, taking her off to a private retreat, and either forcing or seducing her into copulation. The aftermath of this fantasised human encounter was a dimly imagined saga of raw emotions and either an asymmetric interdependence or else brutal abandonment. And out of that tragic encounter was born an infant, destined first to suckle on her mother's breast and eventually to develop into a graceful young woman. Somehow, a relationship of lustful exploitation must have morphed into one in which the merger of two individual lives was appropriated by Gore society as the conception of a new kind of person, endowed with physical traits of both an African and a European genetic lineage. Over the course of history that distinctive brand of physical beauty became a marker of entitlement to certain social privileges. Senegalese society declared "this woman is one of us, not a foreigner, and by virtue of her heritage she is due respect as a *senora,* entitled to exceptional wealth and power".

Yet the cruel context of enslavement from which their earliest conception emerged returned to haunt them and undermine their privileged status when the institution of slavery was abolished in the 19th century, giving rise to a generation of freed slaves. The connotations of the doubly oppressive relationship of male master with female slave became a source of shame. However, in the wake of successive revolutions of gender and ethnic liberation over the 20th century, that shameful history was replaced by an ideal of consensual egalitarian union, celebrated in the 21st century mass media of Hollywood romances, and in sartorial displays of an idealised form of beauty in Senegal's annual Fanal festival.

Boda-boda

Such an evocative, onomatopoeic name! When I first came across it in Kenya, I was reminded of my late father's neologistic name for the noisy motorbikes that disturbed his weekend peace and quiet, at our home in Barnes when I was growing up in the 1950s: the ***bugger-bikes***, as he called them, would rev their engines in a chorus of defiance by their youthful owners as they set out to cruise around our neighbourhood – displaying their manly power, going nowhere in particular but dominating the roads, largely devoid of traffic, and deafening both passers-by and even civilised citizens relaxing at home in their suburban houses or gardens, hoping to enjoy the morning newspaper or a quiet cup of tea.

The name captured his indignation so effectively that I was inspired to explore a way of capping it with some linguistic creativity of my own. One day, when we were *en famille* in what felt like a welcoming ambience, I ventured my joke in response to his light-hearted allusion to the *bugger-bikes* that had just interrupted our conversation. "Have you noticed", I said, "when they are starting up, they go '*fuck, fuck,*

fuck, fuck – bugger, bugger, bugger, bugger' and off they go!" As I looked up to my father (Pa, as we called him) with hope of some smiling appreciation of my apt mimicry, I saw his facial expression cloud. And, as I turned to look at my sister and mother to see what they made of it, I heard him say "Let me never again hear you speak that word in the presence of your mother." It was one of those unexpected moments when the hidden rules of acceptable discourse were starkly revealed to me, causing me irritation and dismay. The intimate culture of our family treasured humour and often seemed excitingly open to exploring new ideas and new forms of expression. The free verse poetry of Dylan Thomas, for instance, would be cited with delight and admiration by Mummy, or Pa would read aloud from his newspaper at Sunday lunch the winning entries in an *invent-a-word* competition (I have never forgotten the word *furge* coined to refer to the stuff that accumulates inside the turn-ups of long trousers). And yet on this occasion it seemed I had violated a taboo. Some days later (or was it months?), when I had recovered from the shock of Pa's severe admonition, I ventured to request an explanation for why the word *bugger* was acceptable in a family joke, but not *fuck*. On the face of it, it seemed that alluding to the activity described in the dictionary as the meaning of *bugger* was significantly more obscene than the activity meant by *fuck*. I don't recall how my father argued his way out of that conundrum. But the term *bugger-bike* has remained part of the vocabulary of our family's intimate culture long after the death of its creator.

So, when I first encountered *boda-bodas* in Kenya, they came with a set of connotations of agreeable onomatopoeia, tinged with aesthetic disgust at the eponymous noise with which they announced their ubiquitous presence across the city and caused me alarm as a pedestrian every time one of them came by, weaving its way through the traffic, ignoring the borders of sidewalks and generally proclaiming a lawless arrogance that led me to keep my distance and avoid making eye-contact with the rider.

But that was all to change as a result of an epiphanic experience between Mombasa and Nairobi in 2018. I had been attending a conference of the Kenya Paediatric Association to discuss the strengths and limitations of the WHO-UNICEF *Nurturing Care Framework (NCF)* for integrating principles of family child-rearing across the challenging interface between cosmopolitan (modern?) professional practices and indigenous African cultural traditions. After the formal conference session, we adjourned to a stimulating dinner conversation, where I shared ideas with a new international colleague from South Africa who had shared the conference platform with me and had somewhat different reservations from mine about the prevailing orthodoxy of the *NCF*. I retired to bed in my seaside hotel, resolved to get up early the next morning and walk down to the shore where I could watch the sun rise over the Indian Ocean.

Before dawn, I packed my belongings, ready for pick-up at the agreed time of 8 by a chauffeur-driven car to take me to Nairobi in time for my flight home to Lusaka, which was scheduled for around midday. Equipped with just my cellphone and clad in shorts and sandals, I sauntered down to the beach and was soaking up the salty, humid air, admiring the view when my phone started ringing. It was an official of the host organisation charged with escorting me to the airport. She advised that my pick-up would be an hour earlier than previously agreed, and warning me to be ready for collection in the hotel lobby in good time, so we could beat the traffic *en route* to Nairobi. So, I would need to get back to my room right now, change into travel clothes, skip breakfast and walk up to the lobby.

As I passed the Reception desk, with my wheelie suitcase in tow, I paused briefly to confirm that I was already checked out, and was greeted by my conference host, who grabbed my travel bags to store them in the boot of the taxi which was already waiting at the foot of the entrance steps. "Let's go," she said, "traffic between here and Nairobi can be quite a problem on Saturday!" Contritely, I installed myself in the back seat, murmuring "I was actually down on the beach when you called -lucky I had my phone with me, and was already packed..." As the driver pulled out into the road, waived on by hotel guards, my host introduced me to another passenger in the front seat, who was a professional in the field of early childhood health, and we plunged into an animated continuation of last night's dinner conversation, in which my host had been a participant. The traffic was indeed congested, but my host assured me that by leaving early we could be confident of reaching the airport by the time scheduled for check-in.

As is my habit on car rides to catch a flight, I ran through a mental check-list of items needed for the trip and realised that when boarding the taxi, I had parted with my jacket containing my travel documents. I knew I had stored my passport and airline ticket in a dedicated plastic travel pouch that fitted comfortably into a pocket of my jacket. But, just to be sure the pouch had made it into the boot of the car, I asked apologetically if the driver could please pull over and allow me to check on my baggage that my host had kindly put in the boot. Oh dear! The pouch was nowhere to be seen in the boot, nor in the seat where I had been relaxing inside the car, engaged in a stimulating academic conversation. Where could it be? Recalling my hurried departure from the hotel room to the lobby, I couldn't visualise the pouch. Evidently, I had not put it into a pocket of my jacket; could I have left it by the bed? "I'm very sorry" I said "- I have to go back to the hotel: I can't board the flight in Nairobi without my passport and ticket." The driver insisted that turning back at this juncture, 30 minutes and several kilometres along the route would make it impossible to reach the airport in time for check-in. Moreover, the other passenger, my conversational partner on issues of child health, was booked on the same flight as me.

Meanwhile, my resourceful host was on the phone to the hotel – could they please check my room to see if I had left behind a pouch containing travel documents? "His name is Professor Serpell, and he was in Room ... What? Oh really? That's wonderful! Please hold." Apparently, my pouch had just been handed in at Reception – found on the floor of the lobby, where it must have dropped out of my baggage just before I got into the taxi. And that was when I heard the word *boda-boda*. A long phone conversation in *kiSwahili* was translated for me as the following plan. The receptionist would contact a known *boda-boda* rider, who would be entrusted with my pouch, and he would follow us, using his flexible driving skills to catch up with our taxi on the way to the airport. I would pay him a modest fee on delivery of my documents in time to check-in to my international flight. My heart, which by this time was in my throat, began to slow down, and the taxi proceeded on its way.

When we reached the perimeter gateway to the airport, our driver explained that *boda-bodas* were not permitted beyond that point. The closing time for check-in was fast approaching, and the *boda-boda* driver had just reported by phone that he was still a few kilometers away. The taxi driver explained our situation to the airport security guard, who agreed with minimal persuasion to make an exception and allow the boda-boda driver to enter, on presentation of his ID (details communicated to us by the hotel). The taxi dropped me and my (now somewhat sympathetic) fellow-traveller at the Departures terminal and went off with our host on their return journey to Mombasa. I explained at the check-in counter that I would be checking in as soon as my passport and ticket were delivered to me. They duly noted that I would be a bit late, while my fellow traveller proceeded into the holding area for passengers about to board.

By the time the *boda-boda* rider called me on my cellphone to announce that he had reached the airport gate and been permitted to drive in, I was sitting alone at a little cafe in the Departures Hall, wondering how much it would cost me to re-book on a later flight, and what I would need to do if the stranger in possession of my passport were to just disappear, deciding to abscond with the dollar notes I had stored in a plain envelope alongside my ticket and passport inside the pouch. The boarding call for my flight was broadcast over the airport loudspeaker system, and I began to lose hope. But then a tall, modestly dressed man emerged from the carpark entrance doorway, casting his eyes around until he spotted me at the cafe, and strode towards me, pouch in hand. I briefly opened it to check that my passport, ticket and -yes!- the envelope were all inside, and gave the rider a few Kenyan banknotes, amounting to double the fee agreed with the hotel. He smiled politely and thanked me for the business. I wanted to hug him as my personal saviour. And for ever since then I have met the eyes of *boda-boda* riders as fellow human beings, despite the dreadful clatter of their infernally dangerous, yet magnificently flexible machines.

Helping a traveler find his way

The word *mlendo* in chiNyanja (aka ciCewa) (literally a *traveler)* *means* a *stranger*, but also a *visitor* and a *guest.* When I first learned this from my teacher Mr F.N. Jere, it struck me as more than a case of linguistic polysemy. It reflects an indigenous cultural norm that prescribes hospitality for strangers in a way that made sense traditionally in rural Chewa society but was somewhat eroded in urban Lusaka as encounters with strangers became more commonplace: how can residents of a crowded city be expected to make every stranger they encounter welcome as a guest?! Travelers' tales have been told by foreign tourists traveling by car in Zambia (and in some other parts of the African continent) recounting how they were received by local villagers when their car broke down "in the middle of nowhere". The random encounter often gave rise to relationships that endured over time, sometimes generating emotional bonds of lasting gratitude by the travelers well beyond their expectations before the accident. In more holistic accounts by Europeans of the quality of personal relationships they find striking in African communities that they have got to know as visitors or sojourners, a recurrent theme is that African societies are welcoming. The idea that a newcomer from outside deserves by definition to be treated helpfully affords opportunities for social bonding that are sadly diminishing in many countries of the modern world faced with an influx of refugees. As I listen from afar to news reports of a growing trend in American politics to construe diversity as threatening to indigenous norms, I am reminded of a heart-warming encounter in 2019 with a modern, urban community that extended assistance to me as a transient visitor.

I was at a loose end in an unfamiliar city. Philadelphia was known to me historically for its early religious tolerance in the 17th century and in the 18th century as the home of Benjamin Franklin, one the founding fathers of the American constitution. But its salient current reputation was as an economically depressed and ethnically polarised conurbation, following an episode in the 1950s of "White flight" from the centre to the suburbs - similar to what had happened in Baltimore, a city I knew well from my extended sojourn there in the 1990s. My time alone in Philadelphia arose between two unrelated appointments. I had scheduled a visit to the home of a friendly cousin I had not seen for years to coincide with his evening return home from work, and my previous get together had ended in the morning as my other friends took off by train from the railway station. So here I was, with my full complement of travel bags packed and ready for tomorrow's journey home to Lusaka by plane. I was glad of a pause between the two events, allowing me time to catch up on my email and perhaps make a few notes about discussions on the previous day. But where could I find a quiet space to read and write, with my travel bags safely stowed? A public library seemed ideal, and with the google map on my phone I located one about half-way between the station and my cousin's home address. My cab driver from the railway station found it, but neither of us could see the building at first, so cozily was it nestled in among similar buildings along the rather folorn streets.

The indoor layout of the library was similar to that of other urban American libraries I had patronised with my children over the years in Baltimore, and I settled down in a corner where I could conveniently stash my bags, open my laptop and connect to the wifi. There was little of interest in my inbox, and I began to look around, noting some familiar titles on the shelves and casually observing the comings and goings of other patrons. Unlike a university library, there was little sense of an obligation to maintain silence. An elderly man who was seated with a patriarchal demeanour in an armchair uttered a cordial, full-volume greeting by name to another elderly patron as he arrived, and they exchanged a few pleasantries. A little girl with golden pigtails gave loud instructions to her motherly escort about which puzzle she wanted to play on the carpeted floor. The woman shushed her and smiled apologetically at the patriarch as she strode away towards the glass exit doors. He nodded and glanced at the child, acknowledging with a smile that she was now fully occupied. The complexions of the protagonists in this relaxed social scenario ranged from chocolate and coffee brown to strawberries and cream, or, as the urban folklore of contemporary America would have it, they included black folks and white folks, as did the library staff.

As the day wore on, I became aware of a pervasive sense of community shared among the member-owners of an intimate micro-culture[6] of regular local patrons and the staff catering to their needs. It was clear to me that I was not a member of that cultural group. But I was effortlessly included as a transient participant. The wifi password to access the internet was handed to me discreetly on a slip of paper by the librarian stationed at the entrance, a big man in his fifties, I guessed from the streaks of grey in his dreadlocks. A young man who had been sitting at a desk quietly gestured to me that I was free to take his place, as he packed up his laptop and left.

As I was getting ready to leave, I realised I was unlikely to find a cab cruising by in this neighborhood. I gathered up my baggage (heavy wheelies for my international journey ahead) thinking it might be a bit exhausting to drag them the 1.5 miles to my next destination. I paused by the friendly librarian who had set me up with guest access to wifi, and asked for advice. He soon appreciated my dilemma. First he

---

[6] The concept of intimate culture was developed in our study of family socialisation of early childhood literacy in urban Baltimore (Serpell, R., Sonnenschein, S., Baker, L., & Ganapathy, H. 2002 *Journal of Family Psychology, 16*, 391-405) and further extended to other social configurations (Serpell, R. 2017. *Perspectives on Psychological Science, 12*, 889-899.)

brought up a google-earth image of the address I was headed for and exclaimed "oh yeah, I know that corner !" He then explained to me that the bus that stopped by the library wouldn't take me there and started brainstorming alternatives, quickly inviting in by their first names two elderly ladies who were just walking in, one black, one white. One of them had the answer and so he wrote down on the back of one of the library's abundant flyers about public transport an agenda of streets to walk along, where to catch the cross-town trolley, which direction to take and where to get off.

I felt a need to share with him how agreeable I had found the atmosphere in his library during my three-hour stay, and said I thought the neighborhood were fortunate to have such a great community resource. He beamed with pleasure, asked me where I was from, and we exchanged a few more pleasantries ("What's it like over there? You know, me I haven't traveled anywhere 'xcept here"). And before I left, he reached out for a big handshake.

I was reminded of an article by my Swiss friend, Francois Rochat, about "common decency", which he believes is what motivated large numbers of ordinary, Christian citizens in one commune of southern France[7] to harbour fugitive Jews during the Nazi occupation.

---

[7] a historical fact that earned the region the award long after the war, by Yad Vashem - The World Holocaust Remembrance Center in DC - of the title "Righteous Among Nations".

In Rochat's essay[8]:

> "Common decency ... is a way of responding to others' difficulties, suffering, and needs, based on kindness; it is a sense of caring for people whose misfortune can be lessened by giving them a hand. Common decency values ordinary life because ordinary life makes room for all of us and is inseparable from all the things that keep life moving forward - all the things that are on the side of our common humanness- and keep us from forgetting about it or neglecting it."

---

[8] Rochat, F. (2018) "When Common Decency Prevails : Rescuers during the Holocaust and Disobedient Subjects in the Milgram Obedience Experiment". *The Journal of the Hannah Arendt Center for Politics and Humanities at Bard College*, Volume 6, 118-126.

www.ingramcontent.com/pod-product-compliance
Lightning Source LLC
Chambersburg PA
CBHW060415050426
42449CB00009B/1971